S0-AVN-194

For

To my brother Gene
and his lovely wife
Enjoy   Lenda
Christmas 1995 Anna Boston

The Miracle *of* Christmas

Compiled by Nick Beilenson

Design by Deborah Michel

PETER PAUPER PRESS, INC.
WHITE PLAINS·NEW YORK

The image of Santa Claus on the jacket is from the private collection of Diane and Ralph Hellebuyck, Old Print Factory, Inc.

Jacket background and interior border illustrations by Grace De Vito

Contents

THE BIRTH OF JESUS CHRIST

The Visit of the Magi

T HIS IS HOW THE BIRTH OF JESUS Christ came about. His mother Mary was pledged to be married to Joseph, but before they came together, she was found to be with child through the Holy Spirit.

Because Joseph her husband was a righteous man and did not want to expose her to public disgrace, he had in mind to divorce her quietly.

But after he had considered this, an angel of the Lord appeared to him in a dream and said, *Joseph son of David, do not be afraid to take Mary home as your wife, because what is conceived in her is from the Holy Spirit. She will give birth to a son, and you are to give him the name Jesus, because he will save his people from their sins.*

All this took place to fulfill what the Lord had said through the prophet: *The virgin will be with child and will give birth to a son, and they will call him Immanuel—which means, God with us.*

When Joseph woke up, he did what the angel of the Lord had commanded him and took Mary home as his wife. But he had no union with her until she gave birth to a son. And he gave him the name Jesus.

After Jesus was born in Bethlehem in Judea, during the time of King Herod, Magi from the east came to Jerusalem and asked, *Where is the one who has been born king of the Jews? We saw his star in the east and have come to worship him.*

When King Herod heard this he was disturbed, and all Jerusalem with him. When he had called together all the chief priests and teachers of the law, he asked them where the Christ was to be born. *In Bethlehem in Judea,* they replied, *for this is what the prophet has written:*

'And you, Bethlehem, in the land of Judah, are by no means least among the rulers of Judah; for out of you will come a ruler who will be the shepherd of my people Israel.'

Then Herod called the Magi secretly and found out from them the exact time the star had appeared. He sent them to Bethlehem and said, *Go and make a careful search for the child. As soon as you find him, report to me, so that I too may go and worship him.*

After they had heard the king, they went on their way, and the star they had seen in the east

7

went ahead of them until it stopped over the place where the child was. When they saw the star, they were overjoyed. On coming to the house, they saw the child with his mother Mary, and they bowed down and worshiped him. Then they opened their treasures and presented him with gifts of gold and of incense and of myrrh. And having been warned in a dream not to go back to Herod, they returned to their country by another route.

When they had gone, an angel of the Lord appeared to Joseph in a dream. *Get up,* he said, *take the child and his mother and escape to Egypt. Stay there until I tell you, for Herod is going to search for the child to kill him.*

So he got up, took the child and his mother during the night and left for Egypt, where he stayed until the death of Herod.

MATTHEW 1:18-2:14 (NIV)

THE CHRISTMAS MIRACLE

 N THE MORNING BEFORE THE Christmas that fell when I was six, my father took my brother and me for a walk in the woods of the Old Colony town where we lived. Three times as we walked he

stopped, and cut a small balsam tree. There was a
very tiny one, hardly more than a seedling; a small
one a foot or so high; and a youthful one of
perhaps four feet. So we each had a tree to bear,
flaglike, back to the house. It didn't occur to us
single-minded larvae that this had the least
connection with Christmas. Our father was a
botanist Ph.D., given to plucking all manner of
specimens whenever we walked, with the offhand
explanation, A *fine* Tsuga canadensis, or whatever
it was. By nightfall we had forgotten all about the
walk.

For this was Christmas Eve, and we were
suddenly in a panic. Where was The Tree? On
experience, we knew that it was usually delivered in
the morning, that Father set it up in the afternoon
and that Mother trimmed it at night, letting us
help with the ornaments before she put us to bed
in a fever of anticipation. But this year we had
seen no tree arrive; look where we would, we could
not find one; and even Mother turned aside our

questions. Would there be no Tree? Would there, perhaps, be no Christmas at all for us? How we wished now, that we had not put the cat in the milk-pail!

But after supper Father and Mother took us into the sitting-room. In a cleared corner over by the big closet stood a jar of earth. *Christmas*, said Father, *is a day of miracles, to remind us of the greatest Miracle of all. Perhaps we shall see one.* Then Mother led us out, closing the door on Father and the jar of earth—and the closet.

We can help, she said, *by learning this song.* And she began, softly but very true, *O Little Town of Bethlehem*. We tried hard in our shrill way. But even Mother had to admit it was only a good try. Yet when the door opened and we went again into the sitting-room, behold! A tiny Tree had appeared in the jar of earth! Hardly more than a seedling, to be sure, and not old enough yet to bear ornaments, but indubitably a Tree. Marveling, we went out again.

This time we did better—on the words, if not the tune. And when we re-entered the sitting-room, the Tree had grown—to perhaps a foot or so in height! A blaze of hope flashed upon us. We went out and tried harder on that song. And sure enough, this time the Tree was taller than either boy. Terrific! We could hardly wait to get outside and sing some more with Mother. For now hope was a rapture of certainty.

To this day I cannot hear *O Little Town of Bethlehem*, from however cracked a curbside organ, without hearing through and beyond it the clear, true voice of my mother. Nor hear that long-vanished sweetness without knowing that presently, somewhere, somehow a great door is going to open and disclose unearthly beauty. It is more than sixty years since our sitting-room door swung back for the fourth time, that night in the Old Colony of Massachusetts. But I can still see, sharp as life, the splendor of the Tree that towered to the ceiling in its glossy dark green, sparkling with silver tinsel, glowing with candles and half hiding in its crisp, fragrant needles, the incomparable perfection of spheres that shone like far-off other worlds, red and blue and green and gold…

Cynics say that miracles are all man-made—contrived, like a Christmas tree hidden in a closet and flashed upon wondering kids. That even the Christmas spirit is only a spell we work up to bemuse one another—and then fall for, ourselves, like so many simple children. What of it? So much the better! If mankind, by its own devoted labor, can induce in itself—if only for a day—an all-pervading spirit of friendship and cheer and good will and loving kindness, that alone is a very great miracle. It is the kind of miracle that must please above all others Him who knows how miracles are wrought.

ROBERT KEITH LEAVITT

13

THE NIGHT
After
CHRISTMAS

 WAS THE NIGHT AFTER CHRISTMAS,
　　when all through the house
　Every soul was abed,
　　　and as still as a mouse;
The stockings,
　　so lately St. Nicholas's care,

Were emptied of all that
       was eatable there.
The Darlings had duly been
       tucked in their beds—
With very full stomachs,
       and pains in their heads.

I was dozing away in my new
       cotton cap,
And Nancy was rather far
       gone in a nap,
When out in the nurs'ry
       arose such a clatter,
I sprang from my sleep, crying—
       What is the matter?

I flew to each bedside—
       still half in a doze—
Tore open the curtains,
       and threw off the clothes;

16

While the light of the taper
    served clearly to show
The piteous plight of
    those objects below;
For what to the fond father's
    eyes should appear
But the little pale face
    of each sick little dear?
For each pet that had crammed
    itself full as a tick,
I knew in a moment now
    felt like Old Nick.

Their pulses were rapid,
    their breathings the same,
What their stomachs rejected
    I'll mention by name—
Now Turkey, now Stuffing,
    Plum Pudding, of course,
And Custards, and Crullers,
    and Cranberry sauce;

17

Before outraged nature,
    all went to the wall,
Yes—Lollypops, Flapdoodle,
    Dinner, and all;
Like pellets which urchins
    from popguns let fly,
Went figs, nuts and raisins,
    jam, jelly and pie,
Till each error of diet
    was brought to my view,
To the shame of Mamma
    and Santa Claus, too.

I turned from the sight,
    to my bedroom stepped back,
And brought out a phial marked
    Pulv. Ipecac.,
When my Nancy exclaimed—
    for their sufferings shocked her—
Don't you think you had better,
    love, run for the Doctor?

18

I ran and was scarcely
       back under my roof,
When I heard the sharp clatter
       of old Jalap's hoof.
I might say that I hardly
       had turned myself round,
When the Doctor came into the room
       with a bound.
He was covered with mud
       from his head to his foot,
And the suit he had on
       was his very worst suit;
He had hardly had time
       to put *that* on his back,
And he looked like a Falstaff
       half fuddled with sack.

His eyes, how they twinkled!
       Had the Doctor got merry?
His cheeks looked like *Port*
       and his breath smelled of *Sherry.*

He hadn't been shaved
    for a fortnight or so,
And the beard on his chin
    wasn't white as the snow.
But inspecting their tongues
    in despite of their teeth,
And drawing his watch
    from his waistcoat beneath,
He felt of each pulse, saying—
    Each little belly
Must get rid—here he laughed—
    of the rest of that jelly.
I gazed on each chubby, plump,
    sick little elf,
And groaned when he said so,
    in spite of myself;
But a wink of his eye when
    he physicked our Fred
Soon gave me to know
    I had nothing to dread.

He didn't prescribe,
> but went straightway to work
And dosed all the rest,
> gave his trousers a jerk,
And, adding directions
> while blowing his nose,
He buttoned his coat;
> from his chair he arose,
Then jumped in his gig,
> gave old Jalap a whistle,
And Jalap dashed off as if
> pricked by a thistle;
But the Doctor exclaimed,
> ere he drove out of sight,
They'll be well by tomorrow—
> *good night, Jones, good night!*

ANONYMOUS **(1861)**

21

UNDER THE MISTLETOE

 ROM THE CENTRE OF THE CEILING of this kitchen, old Wardle had just suspended, with his own hands, a huge branch of mistletoe, and this same branch of mistletoe instantaneously gave rise to a scene of general and most delightful

struggling and confusion; in the midst of which, Mr. Pickwick, with a gallantry that would have done honour to a descendant of Lady Tollimglower herself, took the old lady by the hand, led her beneath the mystic branch, and saluted her in all courtesy and decorum. The old lady submitted to this piece of practical politeness with all the dignity which befitted so important and serious a solemnity, but the younger ladies, not being so thoroughly imbued with a superstitious veneration for the custom: or imagining that the value of a salute is very much enhanced if it cost a little trouble to obtain it: screamed and struggled, and ran into corners, and threatened and remonstrated, and did every thing but leave the room, until some of the less adventurous gentlemen were on the point of desisting, when they all at once found it useless to resist any longer, and submitted to be kissed with a good grace. Mr. Winkle kissed the young lady with the black eyes, and Mr. Snodgrass kissed Emily, and

Mr. Weller not being particular about the form of being under the mistletoe, kissed Emma and the other female servants, just as he caught them. As to the poor relations, they kissed everybody, not even excepting the plainer portion of the young-lady visitors, who, in their excessive confusion, ran right under the mistletoe, as soon as it was hung up, without knowing it! Wardle stood with his back to the fire, surveying the whole scene, with the utmost satisfaction; and the fat boy took the opportunity of appropriating to his own use, and summarily devouring, a particularly fine mince-pie, that had been carefully put by, for somebody else.

Now, the screaming had subsided, and faces were in a glow, and curls in a tangle, and Mr. Pickwick, after kissing the old lady as beforementioned, was standing under the mistletoe, looking with a very pleased countenance on all that was passing around him, when the young lady with the black eyes, after a little

whispering with the other young ladies, made a sudden dart forward, and, putting her arm round Mr. Pickwick's neck, saluted him affectionately on the left cheek; and before Mr. Pickwick distinctly knew what was the matter, he was surrounded by the whole body, and kissed by every one of them.

It was a pleasant thing to see Mr. Pickwick in the centre of the group, now pulled this way, and then that, and first kissed on the chin, and then on the nose, and then on the spectacles: and to hear the peals of laughter which were raised on every side; but it was a still more pleasant thing to see Mr. Pickwick, blinded shortly afterwards with a silk handkerchief, falling up against the wall, and scrambling into corners, and going through all the mysteries of blind-man's buff, with the utmost relish for the game, until at last he caught one of the poor relations, and then had to evade the blind-man himself, which he did with a nimbleness and agility that elicited the admiration and applause of all beholders. The poor relations

caught the people who they thought would like it,
and, when the game flagged, got caught
themselves. When they were all tired of blind-
man's buff, there was a great game of snap-dragon,
and when fingers enough were burned with that,
and all the raisins were gone, they sat down by the
huge fire of blazing logs to a substantial supper,

and a mighty bowl of wassail, something smaller
than an ordinary wash-house copper, in which the
hot apples were hissing and bubbling, with a rich
look, and a jolly sound, that were perfectly
irresistible.

This, said Mr. Pickwick, looking round him,
this is, indeed, comfort.

CHARLES DICKENS,
CHRISTMAS WITH MR. PICKWICK

THE FESTIVAL OF CHRISTMAS

F ALL THE OLD FESTIVALS…THAT OF Christmas awakens the strongest and most heartfelt associations. There is a tone of solemn and sacred feeling that blends with our conviviality, and lifts the spirit to a state of hallowed and elevated enjoyment. The

services of the church about this season are extremely tender and inspiring; they dwell on the beautiful story of the origin of our faith, and the pastoral scenes that accompanied its announcement: they gradually increase in fervor and pathos during the season of Advent, until they break forth in full jubilee on the morning that brought peace and good-will to men. I do not know a grander effect of music on the moral feelings than to hear the full choir and the pealing organ performing a Christmas anthem in a cathedral, and filling every part of the vast pile with triumphant harmony.

It is a beautiful arrangement, also, derived from days of yore, that this festival, which commemorates the announcement of the religion of peace and love, has been made the season for gathering together of family connections, and drawing closer again those bands of kindred hearts, which the cares and pleasures and sorrows of the world are continually operating to cast loose; of calling back the children of a family, who have launched forth in life, and wandered widely asunder, once more to assemble about the paternal hearth, that rallying-place of the affections, there to grow young and loving again among the endearing mementos of childhood....

The pitchy gloom without makes the heart dilate on entering the room filled with the glow and warmth of the evening fire. The ruddy blaze diffuses an artificial summer and sunshine through the room, and lights up each countenance into a kindlier welcome. Where does the honest face of hospitality expand into a broader and more cordial smile—where is the shy glance of love more sweetly eloquent—than by the winter fireside? and as the hollow blast of wintry wind rushes through the hall, claps the distant door, whistles about the casement, and rumbles down the chimney, what can be more grateful than that feeling of sober and sheltering security, with which we look round upon the comfortable chamber, and the scene of

domestic hilarity?

The English, from the great prevalence of rural habits throughout every class of society, have always been fond of those festivals and holidays which agreeably interrupt the stillness of country life; and they were in former days particularly observant of the religious and social rites of Christmas. It is inspiring to read even the dry details which some antiquaries have given of the quaint humors, the burlesque pageants, the complete abandonment to mirth and good-fellowship, with which this festival was celebrated. It seemed to throw open every door, and unlock every heart. It brought the peasant and the peer together, and blended all ranks in one warm generous flow of joy and kindness. The old halls of castles and manor-houses resounded with the harp and the Christmas carol, and their ample boards groaned under the weight of hospitality. Even the poorest cottage welcomed the festive season with green decorations of bay and holly—the cheerful fire glanced its rays through the lattice, inviting the passenger to raise the latch, and join the gossip knot huddled round the hearth, beguiling the long evening with legendary jokes, and oft-told Christmas tales.

WASHINGTON IRVING,
OLD CHRISTMAS

CHRISTMAS;
OR,
THE GOOD
FAIRY

O H, DEAR! *CHRISTMAS IS COMING IN A fortnight, and I have got to think up presents for everybody!* said young Ellen Stuart, *as she leaned languidly back in her chair. Dear me, it's so tedious! Everybody has got everything that can be thought of.*

Oh, no, said her confidential adviser, Miss Lester, in a soothing tone. *You have means of buying everything you can fancy; and when every shop and store is glittering with all manner of splendors, you cannot surely be at a loss.*

Well, now, just listen. To begin with, there's mamma. What can I get for her? I have thought of ever so many things. She has three card cases, four gold thimbles, two or three gold chains, two writing desks of different patterns; and then as to rings, brooches, boxes, and all other things, I should think she might be sick of the sight of them. I am sure I am, said she, languidly gazing on her white and jeweled fingers.

This view of the case seemed rather puzzling to the adviser, and there was silence for a few minutes, when Ellen, yawning, resumed:

And then there's cousins Jane and Mary; I suppose they will be coming down on me with a whole load of presents; and Mrs. B. will send me something—she did last year; and then there's cousins William and Tom—*I must get them something; and I would like to do it well enough, if I only knew what to get.*

Well, said Eleanor's aunt, who had been sitting quietly rattling her knitting needles during this speech, *it's a pity that you had not such a subject to practice on as I was when I was a girl. Presents did not fly about in those days as they do now. I remember, when I was ten years old, my father gave me a most marvelously ugly sugar dog for a Christmas gift, and I was perfectly delighted with it, the very idea of a present was so new to us.*

Dear aunt, how delighted I should be if I had any such fresh, unsophisticated body to get presents for! But to get and get for people that have more than they know what to do with now; to add pictures, books, and gilding when the center tables are loaded with them now, and rings and jewels when they are a perfect drug! I wish myself that I were not sick, and sated, and tired with having everything in the world given me.

Well, Eleanor, said her aunt, *if you really do want unsophisticated subjects to practice on, I can put you in the way of it. I can show you more than one family to whom you might seem to be a very good fairy, and where such gifts as you could give with all ease would seem like a magic dream.*

Why, that would really be worth while, aunt.

Look over in that back alley, said her aunt. *You see those buildings?*

That miserable row of shanties? Yes.

Well, I have several acquaintances there who have never been tired of Christmas gifts or gifts of any other kind. I assure you, you could make quite a sensation over there.

Well, who is there? Let us know.

Do you remember Owen, that used to make your shoes?

Yes, I remember something about him.

Well, he has fallen into a consumption, and cannot work any more; and he, and his wife, and three little children live in one of the rooms.

How do they get along?

His wife takes in sewing sometimes, and sometimes goes out washing. Poor Owen! I was over there yesterday; he looks thin and wasted, and his wife was saying that he was parched with constant fever, and had very little appetite. She had, with great self-denial, and by restricting herself almost of necessary food, got him two or three oranges; and the poor fellow seemed so eager after them.

Poor fellow! said Eleanor, involuntarily.

Now, said her aunt, *suppose Owen's wife should get up on Christmas morning and find at the door a couple of dozen of oranges, and some of those nice white grapes, such as you had at your party last week; don't you think it would make a sensation?*

Why, yes, I think very likely it might; but who else, aunt? You spoke of a great many.

Well, on the lower floor there is a neat little room, that is always kept perfectly trim and tidy; it belongs to a young couple who have nothing beyond the husband's day wages to live on. They are,

41

nevertheless, as cheerful and chipper as a couple of wrens; and she is up and down half a dozen times a day, to help poor Mrs. Owen. She has a baby of her own about five months old, and of course does all the cooking, washing, and ironing for herself and husband; and yet, when Mrs. Owen goes out to wash, she takes her baby, and keeps it whole days for her.

I'm sure she deserves that the good fairies should smile on her, said Eleanor; one baby exhausts my stock of virtues very rapidly.

But you ought to see her baby, said Aunt E.; so plump, so rosy, and so good-natured, and always clean as a lily. This baby is a sort of household shrine; nothing is too sacred or too good for it; and I believe the little thrifty woman feels only one temptation to be extravagant, and that is to get some ornaments to adorn this little divinity.

Why, did she ever tell you so?

No; but one day, when I was coming down stairs, the door of their room was partly open, and I

saw a peddler there with open box. John, the
husband, was standing with a little purple cap on his
hand, which he was regarding with mystified,
admiring air, as if he didn't quite comprehend it, and
trim little Mary gazing at it with longing eyes.

'I think we might get it,' said John.

'Oh, no,' said she, regretfully; 'yet I wish we
could, it's so pretty!'

Say no more, aunt. I see the good fairy must
pop a cap into the window on Christmas morning.
Indeed, it shall be done. How they will wonder where
it came from, and talk about it for months to come!

Well, then, continued her aunt, in the next
street to ours there is a miserable building, that looks
as if it were just going to topple over; and away up in
the third story, in a little room just under the eaves,
live two poor, lonely old women. They are both nearly
on to ninety. I was in there day before yesterday. One
of them is constantly confined to her bed with
rheumatism; the other, weak and feeble, with failing
sight and trembling hands, totters about, her only

helper; and they are entirely dependent on charity.

Can't they do anything? Can't they knit? said Eleanor.

You are young and strong, Eleanor, and have quick eyes and nimble fingers; how long would it take you to knit a pair of stockings?

I? said Eleanor. What an idea! I never tried, but I think I could get a pair done in a week, perhaps.

And if somebody gave you twenty-five cents for them, and out of this you had to get food, and pay room rent, and buy coal for your fire, and oil for your lamp—

Stop, aunt, for pity's sake!

Well, I will stop; but they can't: they must pay so much every month for that miserable shell they live in, or be turned into the street. The meal and flour that some kind person sends goes off for them just as it does for others, and they must get more or starve; and coal is now scarce and high priced.

O aunt, I'm quite convinced, I'm sure; don't run me down and annihilate me with all these terrible realities. What shall I do to play good fairy to these old women?

If you will give me full power, Eleanor, I will put up a basket to be sent to them that will give them something to remember all winter.

Oh, certainly I will. Let me see if I can't think of something myself.

Well, Eleanor, suppose, then, some fifty or sixty years hence, if you were old, and your father, and mother, and aunts, and uncles, now so thick around you, lay cold and silent in so many graves— you have somehow got away off to a strange city, where you were never known—you live in a miserable garret, where snow blows at night through the cracks, and the fire is very apt to go out in the old cracked stove—you sit crouching over the dying embers the evening before Christmas—nobody to speak to you, nobody to care for you, except another poor old soul

45

who lies moaning in the bed. Now, what would you like to have sent you?

O aunt, what a dismal picture!

And yet, Ella, all poor, forsaken old women are made of young girls, who expected it in their youth as little as you do, perhaps.

Say no more, aunt. I'll buy—let me see—a comfortable warm shawl for each of these poor women; and I'll send them—let me see—oh, some tea—nothing goes down with old women like tea; and I'll make John wheel some coal over to them; and, aunt, it would not be a very bad thought to send them a new stove. I remember, the other day, when mamma was pricing stoves, I saw some such nice ones for two or three dollars.

For a new hand, Ella, you work up the idea very well, said her aunt.

But how much ought I to give, for any one case, to these women, say?

How much did you give last year for any single Christmas present?

Why, six or seven dollars for some; those elegant souvenirs were seven dollars; that ring I gave Mrs. B. was twenty.

And do you suppose Mrs. B. was any happier for it?

No, really, I don't think she cared much about it; but I had to give her something, because she had sent me something the year before, and I did not want to send a paltry present to one in her circumstances.

Then, Ella, give the same to any poor, distressed, suffering creature who really needs it, and see in how many forms of good such a sum will appear. That one hard, cold, glittering ring, that now cheers nobody, and means nothing, that you give because you must, and she takes because she must, might, if broken up into smaller sums, send real warm and heartfelt gladness through many a cold and cheerless dwelling, through many an aching heart.

You are getting to be an orator, aunt; but don't

you approve of Christmas presents, among friends and equals?

Yes, indeed, said her aunt, fondly stroking her head. *I have had some Christmas presents that did me a world of good—a little book mark, for instance, that a certain niece of mine worked for me, with wonderful secrecy, three years ago, when she was not a young lady with a purse full of money—that book mark was a true Christmas present; and my young couple across the way are plotting a profound surprise to each other on Christmas morning. John has contrived, by an hour of extra work every night, to lay by enough to get Mary a new calico dress; and she, poor soul, has bargained away the only thing in the jewelry line she ever possessed, to be laid out on a new hat for him.*

I know, too, a washerwoman who has a poor lame boy—a patient, gentle little fellow—who has lain quietly for weeks and months in his little crib, and his mother is going to give him a splendid Christmas present.

48

What is it, pray?

A whole orange! Don't laugh. She will pay ten whole cents for it; for it shall be none of your common oranges, but a picked one of the very best going! She has put by the money, a cent at a time, for a whole month; and nobody knows which will be happiest in it, Willie or his mother. These are such Christmas presents as I like to think of—gifts coming from love, and tending to produce love; these are the appropriate gifts of the day.

But don't you think that it's right for those who have money to give expensive presents, supposing always, as you say, they are given from real affection?

Sometimes, undoubtedly. The Savior did not condemn her who broke an alabaster box of ointment—very precious—simply as a proof of love, even although the suggestion was made, 'This might have been sold for three hundred pence, and given to the poor.' I have thought he would regard with sympathy the fond efforts which human love

49

sometimes makes to express itself by gifts, the rarest and most costly. How I rejoiced with all my heart, when Charles Elton gave his poor mother that splendid Chinese shawl and gold watch! because I knew they came from the very fullness of his heart to a mother that he could not do too much for—a mother that has done and suffered everything for him. In some such cases, when resources are ample, a costly gift seems to have a graceful appropriateness; but I cannot approve of it if it exhausts all the means of doing for the poor; it is better, then, to give a simple offering, and to do something for those who really need it.

Eleanor looked thoughtful; her aunt laid down her knitting, and said, in a tone of gentle seriousness, *Whose birth does Christmas commemorate, Ella?*

Our Savior's, certainly, aunt.

Yes, said her aunt. *And when and how was he born? In a stable! laid in a manger; thus born, that in all ages he might be known as the brother and friend of the poor. And surely, it seems but appropriate to commemorate his birthday by an especial remembrance of the lowly, the poor, the outcast, and distressed; and if Christ should come back to our city on a Christmas day, where should we think it most appropriate to his character to find him? Would he be carrying splendid gifts to splendid dwellings, or would he be gliding about in the cheerless haunts of the desolate, the poor, the forsaken, and the sorrowful?*

And here the conversation ended.

What sort of Christmas presents is Ella buying? said Cousin Tom, as the servant handed in a portentous-looking package, which had been just rung in at the door.

Let's open it, said saucy Will. *Upon my word, two great gray blanket shawls! These must be for you and me, Tom! And what's this? A great bolt of cotton flannel and gray yarn stockings!*

The door bell rang again, and the servant brought in another bulky parcel, and deposited it

on the marble-topped center table.

What's here? said Will, cutting the cord. *Whew! a perfect nest of packages! Oolong tea! oranges! grapes! white sugar!* Bless me, Ella must be going to housekeeping!

Or going crazy! said Tom; *and on my word,* said he, looking out of the window, *there's a drayman ringing at our door, with a stove, with a teakettle set in the top of it!*

Ella's cook stove, of course, said Will; and just at this moment the young lady entered, with her purse hanging gracefully over her hand.

Now, boys, you are too bad! she exclaimed, as each of the mischievous youngsters was gravely marching up and down, attired in a gray shawl.

Didn't you get them for us? We thought you did, said both.

Ella, I want some of that cotton flannel, to make me a pair of pantaloons, said Tom.

I say, Ella, said Will, *when are you going to housekeeping? Your cooking stove is standing down* in the street; 'pon my word, John is loading some coal on the dray with it.

Ella, isn't that going to be sent to my office? said Tom; *do you know I do so languish for a new stove with a teakettle in the top, to heat a fellow's shaving-water!*

Just then, another ring at the door, and the grinning servant handed in a small brown paper parcel for Miss Ella. Tom made a dive at it, and tearing off the brown paper, discovered a jaunty little purple velvet cap, with silver tassels.

My smoking cap, as I live! said he; *only I shall have to wear it on my thumb, instead of my head—too small entirely*, said he, shaking his head gravely.

Come, you saucy boys, said Aunt E., entering briskly. *What are you teasing Ella for? Why, do see this lot of things, aunt! What in the world is Ella going to do with them?*

Oh, I know!

You know! Then I can guess, aunt, it is some

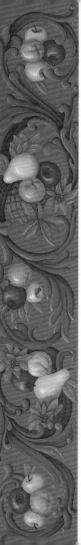

of your charitable works. You are going to make a
juvenile Lady Bountiful of El, eh?

Ella, who had colored to the roots of her
hair at the *exposé* of her very unfashionable
Christmas preparations, now took heart, and
bestowed a very gentle and salutary little cuff on
the saucy head that still wore the purple cap, and
then hastened to gather up her various purchases.

Laugh away, said she, gayly; *and a good
many others will laugh, too, over these things. I got
them to make people laugh—people that are not in
the habit of laughing!*

Well, well, I see into it, said Will; *and I tell you
I think right well of the idea, too. There are worlds of
money wasted, at this time of the year, in getting
things that nobody wants, and nobody cares for after
they are got; and I am glad, for my part, that you
are going to get up a variety in this line; in fact, I
should like to give you one of these stray leaves to
help on,* said he, dropping a ten dollar note into
her paper. *I like to encourage girls to think of*

54

something besides breastpins and sugar candy.

But our story spins on too long. If anybody wants to see the results of Ella's first attempts at *good fairyism*, they can call at the doors of two or three old buildings on Christmas morning, and they shall hear all about it.

HARRIET BEECHER STOWE

A MERRY CHRISTMAS TO YOU